What

G000093370

If you want   effective leader, then this book will show you what you
have to do. By the time you finish reading it, you will
be able to take a broad view of a situation, communicate your analysis to other people, and encourage them
to take the long view. You will also learn how to help
group members articulate for themselves and to other
people how they feel and what they care about, need,
and want and how to attack the problem of change,
growth, or improvement vigorously and enthusiastically.

Other Titles in the Successful Office Skills Series

BECOMING
AN
EFFECTIVE
LEADER

Donald H. Weiss

amacom
American Management Association

New York • Atlanta • Boston • Chicago • Kansas City • San Francisco • Washington, D.C.
Brussels • Toronto • Mexico City

This publication is designed to provide accurate and authoritative
information in regard to the subject matter covered. It is sold with
the understanding that the publisher is not engaged in rendering
legal, accounting, or other professional service. If legal advice or
other expert assistance is required, the services of a competent professional person should be sought.
Library of Congress Cataloging-in-Publication Data

Weiss, Donald H., 1936–
    Becoming an effective leader / Donald H. Weiss.
        p.   cm. — (The successful office skills series)
    Includes bibliographical references and index.
    ISBN 0-8144-7816-6
    1. Leadership.   I. Series.
    HD57.7.W453   1993
    658.4'092—dc20   93-4119
                                                    CIP

Printing number

10   9   8   7   6   5   4   3   2   1

CONTENTS

EVERYONE A LEADER. That slogan at a well-known international corporation headquartered in St. Louis is intended to instill pride and encourage quality among its employees. Yet to some, the slogan trivializes the concepts of leader and leadership. So in this book I recast the slogan to say that everyone *can become* a leader able to meet the needs of the group in a manner appropriate to his or her own needs, style, and strengths.

Leadership is not a subject to treat lightly. Thousands of writers have addressed it ever since civilization began. The *Story of Rama*, from ancient India, extols the heroic qualities of the leader Rama. The ancient Greek philosopher Plato, in his *Republic*, examines the leadership qualities of the Republic's Guardians. And every year magazines publish over a thousand articles about the subject. Yet people are not much closer now to agreeing on the meaning of leader and leadership than they ever were.

To some, expertise is the distinguishing trait of the leader. To others, it's style or charisma. To still others, it's the ability to influence people or persuade them to do something, or the ability to communicate a vision, or the ability to build coalitions among people. On the other hand, maybe *all* these characteristics define the leader.

By definition, of course, a leader is someone who has followers. But, that truism raises other questions, not the least of which is the ethical question of whether or not Hitler and other people whose histories raise ugly images were leaders. Most people would reluctantly agree that, yes, they were leaders—albeit devilishly vile leaders. They did have followers, and, by definition, that made them leaders.

Images of dynamic and exciting leaders have led

even so-called authorities in the field to claim that leaders have a mysterious, inborn power to lead. And some people do have more ebullience than others—a greater vitality that invests what they do with what people call charisma. Yet the world is full of leaders, most of whom are drawn reluctantly into their roles by circumstances.

Therefore, a basic assumption of this book is that leaders are made, not born. The question we answer is how an ordinary person can become an effective leader.

CHAPTER ONE

Traits That Can Make You a Leader

In practice, we can agree on many things about leaders—not only that, by definition, they have followers, but also that they exhibit a number of traits that people look for, admire, and would emulate if they could.

Traits of Effective Leadership

The following list, only partial at best, represents the characteristics most commonly mentioned when people talk about leadership.

- The ability to see the whole picture
- The ability to communicate the whole picture to other people
- The ability to interpret and articulate the group's needs, aspirations, and feelings

- Concern and respect for individual needs, aspirations, feelings, and abilities within the group
- The ability to communicate the group's needs, aspirations, and feelings to people outside the group
- A grasp of what people need or want for themselves
- The ability to inspire people to do what they otherwise might not do for themselves or for others
- The ability to provide people with direction and to focus people's energies on specific goals while maintaining high group morale
- Enthusiasm for the group's mission, objectives, and standards
- An avid desire for change, growth, or improvement
- The energy necessary for conducting the business of the group

As you read that list of characteristics, you probably thought of many different people, ranging from your parents to John F. Kennedy, Nelson Mandela, Mohandas Gandhi—and, yes, Adolf Hitler. You can add anyone else you like to that list. The best-known names that come to mind embody most, if not all, of the enumerated characteristics, which anyone aspiring to leadership would do well to emulate.

Leaders Are What You Think They Do

A common thread running through the entire list of leadership traits is that they all suggest action. Attributes such as blue eyes or tallness are conspicuous by their absence. We talk about leaders *doing* things, rather than *having* blue eyes or *being* tall. A leader may have blue eyes, but she is noteworthy because of what she does—because "she seems to know what's going on" or because "she turned me on to doing things I wouldn't have otherwise done." A leader may be tall, but we respond to him because "he tells it like it is" or "he's willing to fight City Hall—win, lose, or draw." What we perceive that people do or what we feel about their actions makes them leaders in our own eyes.

Even when we say things like "She's a kind person," we're referring to what she did that makes us think she's kind: helping a new employee overcome his reluctance to speak up or giving you a hand in getting out a major project, sacrificing her own work and free time to help. When people do or say things you value, you respond positively to them. In turn, your reactions to them help them become leaders.

In this book, a leader is defined as someone people perceive as:

- Exemplifying the traits of leadership
- Holding beliefs, values, or attitudes with which people agree or to which people respond positively
- Doing things that people admire and would emulate if they could

All that is true of the people who came to mind when you read the list of traits earlier. But I'm not going to talk about any of those people, because we rarely find ourselves in the presence of these larger-than-life figures or have the opportunity to become leaders of their stature. Instead, we usually deal with people in the businesses where we work, in the communities in which we live, and in the daily comings and goings of ordinary life.

So, to talk about how you can become an effective leader, I'm going to draw a composite image that is based on many men and women I've known who exemplify the traits of leadership to which most people seem to respond. Although her description is drawn from real-life experience, this composite leader is not a specific person whom you can identify. She reflects ordinary people doing the ordinary things that make up a person's life.

Dana O'Brien, just completing her eighth year at Wilson Publications, Inc., an independent (but international) publishing house, is the supervisor of one of its sales support groups. We find her faced with the plight of many supervisors in downsized companies: the need to do more with less.

In order to turn around the previous year's poor profit picture, the company has asked for cutbacks across the board, and Dana has to lay off two people from her unit. The company also has provided additional incentives to salespeople and distributors to increase sales. That puts extraordinary pressure on Dana's group.

While I hope that story will be interesting (it, too, is based on a composite of real events), I want you to apply it to yourself. Even if you're not a supervisor, you too can become a leader, so put yourself in Dana's shoes whenever you can. Answer questions like "What would I do in her place?," "How could I get the information I need for doing this?," "How would I delegate responsibility for what has to happen?," and "How could I find out how people are feeling about things?" Only by looking at the story as if you were in it will the lessons be useful to you. Anyone can become a leader if he or she assumes a leadership role.

A lot of people may read our list of traits in this chapter and ask, "Do I have what it takes to be a leader?" But that's the wrong question. Rather, ask yourself, "What do I have to do to become a leader?" That's a much easier question to answer.

To help you answer it, we provide step-by-step explanations of ways you develop leadership skills. In the Appendix, you'll find a short questionnaire that will help you find out if you are already conducting yourself as a leader. Turn to the Appendix now. Complete the exercise and read the interpretation before reading on.

CHAPTER TWO

Seeing the Big Picture

❧

Leaders rarely look at their world as a closed or limited circle with little or no relationship to anything and anyone around it. And they rarely feel altogether satisfied with the way things are; instead, they ask for what could or should be. Leaders look at the big picture and feel uncomfortable with what is. That, in part, is what separates them from followers.

Many people can qualify as leaders on these terms. No one knows who they are, however, because they don't take the essential second step that all leaders take: communicating their perceptions or vision to other people. When you can both see the big picture and communicate what you see, you are on your way to becoming an effective leader.

Seeing the Whole Picture

Most people promoted into supervisory positions come up through the ranks as doers: They make things, operate machines, sell goods, or provide services. As the old joke goes, "Yesterday I couldn't spell *supervisor.* Today I are one."

Most people promoted that way can usually do an acceptable job of managing their work unit—keeping work flowing, administering the budget, keeping records, and watching over quality. Appointed as supervisors, they have the support of their managers and their employees—most of the time and until trouble starts.

Trouble can show up as anything from increased tardiness to missed deadlines or increased waste or horrendous quality or unacceptably low levels of productivity—symptoms of underlying difficulties that good administrators may not be able to handle and may, in fact, be responsible for creating. Often, administrators create their own difficulties by failing to grasp the overall direction of the organization and how their unit fits into it. As a result, they fail to see the nature of their own responsibilities, including helping their employees grasp what is happening around them and to them. In short, although they manage well, they fail to lead.

Leaders do what Dana O'Brien has to do today—walk out of a management meeting, lay off two people, and convince her remaining staff that the layoff will benefit everyone. To do that she has to understand the needs of the organization as a whole and the way in which her particular unit can best serve those needs.

Dana sits on the edge of her chair as she talks with her manager, Stu Borman. They have just returned to his office from a large management meeting, and the shock of what she has heard has begun to wear off.

Dana: Let's make sure I have this straight. According to the top brass, during the last three quarters, we lost a quarter of a million dollars?

Stu: I'm afraid so. You heard it right. Flat sales, steeply increasing costs. I know you have a thorough sense of what it takes to take a book from concept to delivery.

Dana: Well, sure. I knew sales were off, but not by that much. [*Dana sits back in her chair, resigned to the company's realities.*] I shouldn't be so surprised. I read in the paper that book reading has slipped. Well, the meeting certainly opened my eyes to a lot of things. I don't know if my people will understand it. They'll think it's just another way for the owners to line their own pockets.

Stu: They're taking a hit, too. Unlike other top bosses I know of, they're not just deferring their income, they're actually cutting it. That's pretty rare.

Dana: I'll say, and it'll help me sell the plan to the four who survive this cut. You know that the demand for more with less will go over like a bowl full of poison.

Stu: Who will you cut?

Dana: I don't know yet. There's not one of them I don't need. I've cross-trained everyone except for Stan's job. No one in the group has his background for keeping the machines running.

Rose is close to retirement. She's a candidate for early retirement, but I don't know if she'll go for it. She'll take a big cut in benefits if she accepts it. Besides, after fifteen years in this department, she knows more about our salespeople and customers than anyone else. She would be a terrible loss, I can tell you.

Alan is the most recently hired, and he's probably the most expendable right now because I don't think he can pick up the slack if I let other people go.

I'm going to ask for volunteers to take the two-month severance package. If no one goes for it, I'll offer Rose early retirement and let Alan go.

Stu: Let me know what's going on. We need it all
            settled by Thursday noon.

Dana spends the few minutes walking back to her
office and ponders how to break the news. Of seven
people, two have to go. Who? Rose Carney, their word-
processing dynamo due to retire in two years? Alan
Frank, hired less than a year ago, up and coming, with
a pregnant wife and a two-year-old to support? Patty
Jones, her star customer service rep, with two children
to support on her own? Stan Adams, the computer
whiz without whom all their work would crash and
burn given any serious catastrophe and on whom the
salespeople rely for continual communication between
the field and the home office? Francine Strauss, the salespeople's favorite support person, the one on whom
they all call to get their orders processed immediately?
Sally Fried, whose nimble fingers on the calculator
keep the salespeople's records and billings current?
Herself? *Maybe,* Dana thinks, *maybe I'm as expendable as
anyone else.*

Dana starts her staff meeting.

Dana: I don't know any other way to break bad
            news than to be open and honest, straight-
            forward. You've heard by now that the
            company has lost nearly a million dollars
            during the first three quarters of the year.
            Forecasts for the last quarter aren't favor-
            able. To be honest, if we don't make some
            serious changes, we face bankruptcy.
            We've always operated close to the margin
            in order to guarantee the best books, the
            highest-quality products, and the best ser-
            vice in our niche in the industry. That de-
            votion to quality has cost us, but we think
            it's worth it. And we think it's worth our
            while to make the changes we have to

make—because management's optimistic that we can turn it around next year.

We will continue to produce high-quality products and publish only the very best books in spite of some money-saving changes in how we do business. But we can survive only if we make real sacrifices now in order to come back later.

Rose [*sarcastically*]: *Who* are we going to sacrifice?

Dana: Everyone's sacrificing something, and we don't want to hurt anyone.

Rose: Everyone?

Dana: Everyone. The owners announced at the meeting that they, too, will cut their personal incomes, their perks, and their staffs. They've asked us all to make 10 percent cuts in our budget requests. For us to do that in this department, we're going to have to cut out two salaries.

Rose: Oh, boy. Here it comes.

Sally: C'mon, Rose. Give Dana a break. Let's hear her out.

[*Alan sits stiffly in his chair. As the last hired, he figures to be the first fired.*]

Alan: What's the deal?

Dana: We have seven people in this unit, including me, and we have to cut back to five by the end of the month. Three weeks from today. I don't want to be arbitrary and throw darts at a personnel board. You all have families to support and personal needs to meet, and you've all done excellent work. There's no one here I want to lay off.

So I'm asking for volunteers to take a

two-month severance package. No one gets more or less. If you have ten years or more in the company, you get an extra lump sum bonus of $500 for every year of service. Benefits stay in effect for the two months and can be rolled over to your own responsibility under the COBRA laws. That's the best we can offer except for, in your case, Rose, early retirement.

Francine: That's the deal?

Dana: That's it. You have a few days to think about it. Take into consideration that those who stay on won't have an easy time of it. We're going to have to work harder with fewer people and fewer resources. It'll be a challenge. Are you willing to accept that challenge, and are you up to it?

I need answers by 10 o'clock, Thursday. The first two people to volunteer get the package. If there are no volunteers, I'll have to choose and submit my report by noon that day. The company will do whatever we can to help—letters of reference, leads if we get any. We'll print résumés for you and give you time off to interview during your two-week notice period. Helen Gallagher in personnel is putting together a memo on how to write a resume, how to file for unemployment insurance, and how to apply for insurance under COBRA.

I never thought I could see things this way. I always thought that you'd all stay in the company until you chose to leave. You're all the best, and I don't consider any of you expendable. And I'll miss anyone who leaves.

I think all of us supervisors feel the

same way. No one feels good about doing this, but we all understand how important it is for the company that we do it. We all believe that it's the right thing to do. Now, all we ask is that you also understand the situation and cooperate.

The "right thing to do." That's usually at the core of a leader's vision. Whatever the vision may be, it's the right thing as far as the leader is concerned. He is committed to it, no matter what the consequences to his own life, because he believes in it. And more than that, he is able to articulate that vision and communicate it to other people in a way that they can grasp it and sense its rightness, too.

Dana has experienced what we call a "paradigm shift"—a new way of perceiving the world. She now sees the company's situation from a different perspective and with a renewal of intellectual and emotional energy focused on a principle. This transformation is brought on by a vision involving values and new measures of what is right. Dana O'Brien is now a different person, doing something she would not have done had she not seen a revised picture of what is right for the company.

Lay off people if you have to. Dana didn't initiate the idea, but she now takes ownership of it. Her new vision of the facts and realities of the company is clearly not neutral or plain vanilla. It's heavily laden with values—what is good for the company, what is good for the unit, what is good for the individuals involved.

Yet facts and realities underlie what Dana and the others see. The company is losing money and can't pay all the salaries without losing more money and, possibly, facing bankruptcy; that's a fact and a reality. The managers have considered the facts and have found issues to confront; they are prepared to confront them with appeals to both reason and emotion. Realities and values mark all perceptions of the total picture. You can't have one without the other.

Communicating the Big Picture to Others

As I mentioned, you must communicate your vision to other people. If you aspire to leadership, you have to articulate your perception in ways that other people can grasp. That means more than just reciting facts.

Facts by themselves do not move people to action, although facts are essential ingredients for communication. You have to invest the facts with values that convey an awareness of the needs, aspirations, and emotions that infuse your vision.

Had Dana not been able to communicate the rightness of the decisions to her people, she could never have become a leader. Her little speech to her staff was spontaneous and unrehearsed, yet it expressed her perceptions in everyday terms that everyone could understand and with a genuine concern for everyone's needs, aspirations, and feelings—as well as for her own. She summarized both the company's and her staff's needs, aspirations, and feelings. She evoked a positive response even from the sarcastic Rose.

The next morning, at 8:05 A.M., to be exact, Rose knocks on Dana's cubicle door frame.

Rose: Can I come in?
Dana: Sure. How are you this morning?
Rose: Disturbed. I tossed and turned most of the night. Drove my husband nuts, but he's nuts anyway, so it doesn't matter. [*Rose and her husband have just celebrated their twenty-eighth anniversary, and no one ever takes her comments about her husband seriously.*] We figured I'd go

ahead and volunteer for early retirement. It's the right thing to do and the only way I can help this company survive. You made quite a speech yesterday, and it made me realize that I've got too much of me invested in this company to see it go under.

Less than ten minutes after Dana sends Rose to Helen Gallagher in personnel to further discuss what early retirement entails (especially the legal implications), Alan knocks on Dana's cubicle door frame.

Alan: I thought about what you said yesterday, about sacrificing and everything. It's not going to be any picnic around here after two of us are gone, and, because I'm the least expert at the job, I'll only be a drag on the others. I'll take the package and take my chances out there.

Dana: We'll help all we can.

Alan: I know. I couldn't have made this decision if I didn't believe you. I'm glad the baby's due next month. It'll still be covered under this policy.

Relieved that the two people she would have chosen to lay off self-selected, Dana submits her report. And she adds something to it that no one in management above her expects:

My cuts were made easily by the good graces of the people who agreed to leave. The department's ability to produce at current or higher levels will depend on the good graces of the people who remain and on the good graces of those of us in management to give these people all the support we can. We will make outrageous demands on them as well as on ourselves, and, unless we manage them with kindness and consideration, we will lose them, too—probably when we can least afford it.

When leaders address the converts, the applause is rewarding, but that's the easy part of leadership. To become an effective leader, you need to put yourself in a position to reach other people, to communicate your vision to them. Dana's work as the leader has only just begun. She must now interpret and articulate the group's needs, aspirations, and feelings, not only for and to the people in her group but also to others.

CHAPTER THREE

Identifying With the Group

Empathy. *Webster's Dictionary* defines this word as "the power to enter into the feeling or spirit of others." That is, leaders identify with their followers, and they demonstrate their empathy by listening to, respecting, interpreting, and articulating the group's needs, aspirations, and feelings.

Empathy

Looking into the heart of the concept, you see that empathy requires the ability to take in the big picture—that is, the overall situation—of individuals or of a group, to understand what others think and how they feel. Dana took in the big picture affecting each person she had to lay off. She also took in the big picture for each "survivor," considering how, as a group, the survivors would manage what she called "outrageous demands." She weighed the good of the company as a whole against the good of each person and of the group. She listened to the people whose lives her decisions affected and understood how her decisions would affect each one of them, as well as the department. Then she walked the mile in their moccasins to understand their thoughts and feelings.

That identification didn't cause her to freeze, as some people believe it might. Rather, it helped her do what she had to do—ask for volunteers, but be ready to make the hard decisions herself if she had to.

Listening

Identifying with what other people think or feel begins by listening to them. If others perceive you to be a listener, they will tell you what they think or feel. It's a circular process that reinforces itself: People talk, and you listen; listen, and people will talk. But the word *listen* is a metaphor; it represents *any* way of observing people—seeing what they do, watching how they express themselves, studying what they produce. It's the way in which you take in the big picture of a person.

To become an effective leader, you have to listen to people. Listen to their complaints. Listen to their ideas. Listen to their advice and counsel. This doesn't mean that you can just sit there like a lump, eyes glazed over, nodding or saying "Uh huh" periodically. You have to really listen—actively listen. Clear the deck, be open to what people say, ask questions, study body language, acknowledge, give feedback, and summarize.

Seven Rules for Active Listening

1. *Clear the deck.* You actively listen by clearing your desk and your mind of anything that could get in

the way. Think about something else, or think about how you should respond, and you aren't listening.

2. *Be open.* Let the other person say what she has to say, regardless of what it is, whether it pleases you or not. Defensiveness, guardedness, refusing to listen to unpleasant things—these close down communication. Why should anyone listen to you, if you won't listen to her?

3. *Ask questions.* Fully understand what the other person is saying to you, and make sure you understand by asking questions for clarification or for elaboration: "What do you mean?" or "Would you tell me more about that?"

4. *Study body language.* People "talk" with their tone of voice, with their eyes, with their hands, with their posture. And what they "say" in these ways usually communicates what they feel even more than their words do. Learn how to "listen" to body language. While some signals have universal meaning (for example, leaning into the conversation suggests interest or eagerness), people also send signals unique to themselves, signals that you have to learn how to decode: "I know you're tense about this, Alan, from the way you're squeezing that notebook in your hand. I've seen you do that before."

5. *Acknowledge.* Let the other person know you understand, and especially let him know you understand his feelings: "I see what you mean about the insurance, and I realize how bad it would be for you if you lost it before the baby is born."

6. *Give feedback.* Paraphrase what the other person says: "So, you'll take the early retirement." Reflect her feelings: "That's a tough decision for you to make. I can see the strain in your face and hear it in your voice."

7. *Summarize.* Before moving forward or changing

the subject, make sure the other person has finished: "Okay. So you'll take the severance package. You'll put together a résumé for Helen to edit, and I'll write a letter of reference. Anything else?"

Really listening is the only way you can understand what other people are thinking and feeling. And only when you understand them can you identify with them.

Showing Concern

Just understanding what people say means little. You can understand everything perfectly well, yet not care. Without caring, you can't empathize. To become an effective leader, you have to demonstrate a concern for the needs, aspirations, and feelings of the group. (Notice that word *demonstrate*; saying you care won't make it so.)

Empathy implies a degree of detachment. That's how you distinguish empathy from sympathy or pity. You don't have to feel *the other person's* emotions to understand that she feels bad or good. But you need to have your own feelings. What difference does it make to someone if you merely understand without feeling or caring? You must feel deeply for and about the people you lead and about each individual in the group. Without this connection, a leader cannot communicate the group's needs, aspirations, and feelings.

These feelings have to be real. Without real feelings, the leader comes across as insincere. "I'm excited," said in a flat voice, is far less believable than the same words said in an upbeat, energetic tone. Saying "I feel bad for you" but not doing anything to help alleviate the pain or the stress rings hollow.

You will lose your followers' support and loyalty unless you demonstrate support and loyalty to them.

Dana shows us the way when she discusses the situation with Alan.

Dana: I'll do everything I can to help you. I know a couple of people—here, I'll write down their names and phone numbers—I want you to talk to. They might not have anything for you, but they can help you start networking. I'll put in a good word for you, too.

She can't save Alan's job, but she can help him find another one.

Showing Respect

Dignity and self-esteem are at the heart of the human spirit and define respect. You sustain your position as a leader by respecting the rights, needs, aspirations, feelings, and abilities of each person, accepting their differences as well as their conformity to the standards of the group. Also, respecting their unique value as individuals nurtures their willingness to follow you.

The respect between you and other people defines you as a leader. Without it, people may do as you tell them—they may be compliant or obedient—but they'll have no commitment to you or to what has to be done. Without commitment, there's no loyalty. Without loyalty, there's no leadership.

Dana: Alan, you're a good worker and a fine person. I hate to see you leave, but it's probably best that you do. If we look at this as an opportunity, we'll be able to parlay your experience here into an even better position with well-defined career potential. You'll land on your feet and land running.

Concern and respect help a person feel good about himself and about you, even in the worst circumstances.

Communicating Openly

Just as communicating your perception of the big picture helps separate you as a leader from nonleaders, so too does your ability to communicate the group's needs, aspirations, and feelings, both in and out of the group.

Effective leaders talk knowledgeably and sincerely with individual members of the group.

Dana: Stan, I'm going to have to ask you to take on some extra duties. I know that you spend most of your time producing the sales reports. You also spend a lot of time debugging the software and helping the others solve problems with their computers, but we also need you to handle telephone inquiries. That's a lot to ask, but you know the situation. So, let's talk about the best way to handle this. Tell me what you think and feel about it.

Effective leaders not only work easily and comfortably with individuals, they also address the whole group and strike respondent chords.

Dana: The situation's now clear. The five of us have to pick up the slack. And that's a tough task, now that sales are increasing.

Francine: Faster than I thought they would.

Dana: That's causing some difficulties, isn't it?

Francine [*laughing*]: You always were a master of understatement. Yeah, the phones are backing up. We're putting people on hold for too long.

Dana: Other than hiring more people, what do you recommend we do?

Patty [*pulling a catalogue out of a file folder*]: I think we can answer that with a gizmo I saw in this catalogue. Stan, can you install this in our voice-mail system? [*She pushes the catalogue across the table to the techni-cian.*] It'll help expedite the traffic.

You get the picture by now. Dana didn't go to Francine and then to Patty and then to Stan to talk about and solve problems in the unit. She sat down with the whole group, comfortable with the role of facilitator, rather than problem-solver. She raised the issues (struck a respondent chord) and let the group work on possible solutions without feeling threatened by the group's initiative or creativity. And Patty exercised her leadership skills by taking the initiative, offering information, and moving the group toward a solution to its problem.

But Dana can't stop here. Before she can assume the mantle of leader, she has to articulate and communicate the group's messages to outsiders so that outsiders can grasp the messages easily.

Dana: Stu, they're swamped by the phone. Francine and Patty, in particular.

Stu: Sales improved a lot, haven't they?

Dana: More than anyone had expected. Now no one's complaining about that. And no one's asking if we can rehire Rose or Alan. No, they're asking for two things. One, patience on the part of the salespeople. They need to know what's happening here. Once they do, they won't think we've got it in for them when we ask them to call back or put them on hold. One of them said some pretty rude and crude things to Francine yesterday, even though she wasn't rude to him. I heard her side of the conversation and know she was patient and as helpful as she could be. Please, what can you do?

Stu: I'll talk with Jack and his sales managers. Most of them understand what you're experiencing, but some of them see every minute as another dollar out of their pockets. We'll send them a memo explaining the situation. Also, how about you coming to the sales meeting next month to talk it over with them?

Dana: Sounds like a good idea. Now, to control the customers, Patty's found this phone message relay system in this catalogue. Stan says he can install it, so it'll cost $500 to buy but nothing extra to install. He says he can install it in about an hour. That's all the down time it'll take. Five hundred dollars and one hour, and it'll save us frayed nerves, many thousands of dollars, and quite a few hours.

Stu: The extra money's a problem. We don't have much fat in the budget. But go ahead and do it. We'll find the extra five hundred somewhere. Your department's done so much to help out, I'm sure no one will object to this.

Both Dana and Patty could have backed out of the solution to the problem altogether. Patty didn't have to look for a solution to the problem; she could have let someone else do it. Dana could have said, "No. We can't spend any extra money now," when Patty wanted to spend $500. Neither one of them had to do anything; yet they both recognized the group's needs, accepted all the realities of their situation, and did what they believed was right. That's leadership.

CHAPTER FOUR

Influencing People

If you're a supervisor or manager, you have power— that is, you have control over the lives of other people and the rewards for which they work. It comes with the territory. But having that kind of power—we call it *status power*—is not synonymous with influence.

You can influence people even if you don't have status power. This kind of influence is what we call *personal power*—giving other people direction, gaining their commitment and loyalty, transforming their values and beliefs (their "vision"), and moving them to action. To do all that, you have to be focused on the group's goals. Only then will others see you as their leader, rather than as an opportunist taking advantage of a situation in which you may or may not have status power.

Types of Power

Your status or influence within the group gives you the appearance of power, even if you don't really have any at all outside the group. However, the people inside your group invest you with the power that you have. Other people may or may not recognize that power. In fact, leaders don't always have power, especially at the start of whatever it is they lead.

Status power is the authority invested in you by virtue of your position—especially since it's through status power that you control available benefits, rewards, and results of action. Personal power, however, emerges as people see you get things done, see that you can and do influence other people and events, and see you exercise control over yourself.

Some people have status power but not personal power; others have personal power but not status power. Dana had neither when she went before the sales group. Her status and personal power extended only within her own unit. And the sales group hardly knew her and couldn't know what kind of personal power she had. It knew only that she supervised a group that the sales group was beginning to recognize as "them" (at best) and often as "the enemy." She then had to earn her stripes, as they say. She had to influence or persuade members of the sales group, to provide direction or guidance. She had to exercise personal power.

Tapping Into Motivation

You don't motivate others. Motivation comes from the inside. It's what you feel or value; it's what stirs you to action.

Effective leaders grasp this point. They look into each person to discover what that individual needs or wants. They make a sincere effort to understand individual needs, aspirations, and feelings through observing, communicating, and probing.

Observing: You need to use your powers of observation when watching people. See what makes them smile and what discourages them. Make a note to yourself, on paper if you have to, when something excites people. Look steadily into their eyes as they talk about things that make them unhappy; read the signs of pain and discomfort you find there. Over time, you will learn to identify the key motivators that drive them.

Many effective leaders lack textbook knowledge, and much of what they do is intuitive. They don't think about it. They just do it.

Communicating: Even if you don't have textbook answers to what motivates people, you can talk with them. Listen to what they say about themselves, what they like and don't like, how they feel about things, especially about their work, you, and the organization. This way you draw out the information you need.

Francine: Thanks for going to bat for us. [*Dana is getting ready to go to the sales meeting where she intends to put the sales support team's case before the salespeople.*] It means a lot to us.

Dana: I haven't done anything yet.

Francine: Yes, you have. You've listened. You've understood. You're sticking out your neck. Again, thanks. [*Francine starts out the cubicle but stops and turns around.*] Hiring another person wouldn't mean as much as your support.

Probing: Probe when necessary, either directly or indirectly. It's not prying to ask people about what they like and don't like. Too often, we allow a crucial moment to slip away when all that's necessary is to ask a simple question.

Dana: I really appreciate that, Francine. But help me to understand. What makes this meeting so important? Another pair of hands would certainly relieve the pressure here.

Francine: Hey! Don't get me wrong. We'd love another person, but we know it's not possible now. But what would our lives be like if you didn't care that we're sweating bullets here? We know you're trying to help.

Dana: And that I'm trying is important to you.

Francine: And to everyone else. We like what you're doing, Dana. Everyone of us will do whatever we have to do to help you.

Probing encourages people to talk with you. It shows them that you are really interested in them. But you have to probe appropriately; unless they're job-related, people's thoughts or feelings are off limits.

Encouraging

You can encourage people in ways other than by probing. All effective leaders are encouragers. You can encourage people by helping them see that they can benefit by doing what you want. Another way to
encourage people to do what they otherwise might not
do for themselves or for others is by rewarding them for
what they do.

WIIFM: That's pronounced "whiff 'em" and stands for
What's in it for me?—a well-known principle of leadership. People are more likely to respond to your influence if you can help them see the benefits for themselves in what you want from them. Probing helps you
find out their WIIFMs.

Dana [*beginning her presentation to the sales group*]:
Given our situation, what do you need from us
the most? How can we be of greatest help?
[*She writes the sales group's answers on a flip chart
until the flurry of answers dies down.*] What else?
When no one answers, she divides the list into
three categories: "Can Do," "Will Try To Do,"
and "Can't Do." Then she goes over each item,
identifying what her group can do with no extra effort and what it can do only with great
effort.

Dana [*before talking about the items in the last list, the
shortest of the three*]: So we'll work with you on
all of these things in the "Can Do" and "Try To
Do" lists—meeting your needs the best we can.
But, like you, we have needs as well. To help
you most effectively, you have to help us help
you. These are things we just can't do under
the circumstances and until the circumstances
change.

People, we each, as individuals, have our

own needs to meet. You salespeople have sales to make, quotas to fill, commissions to earn. You each contribute to the group's overall sales goals, and when you exceed them, you divide the bonus money. Well, we, in our group, have the same sales goals to meet—as well as our individual standards and objectives. We're on the same sales team you are and share in the sales team's bonus. Only by working together can we all reach these common goals. That's also the way we each realize what's in it for us as individuals and as a group. In our part of the team, we need help. . . . [*At this point, one of the salespeople interrupts, volunteering what he sees as a common goal and ways in which all the salespeople can help to achieve it. That prompts other people to speak up. Before long, Dana fills several flip charts with ideas that have come from the sales group rather than from herself.*]

Her probing and her clear and sincere responses have helped uncover the benefits to the salespeople of working together with her group to solve mutual problems and to reach common goals.

Rewarding: You can't expect people to sustain their motivation if they feel unappreciated. You have to reward them for conforming to the vision you've imparted to them. You have to reinforce good feelings within the group and for the group and provide incentives for people to go on, especially when the going is difficult, as Dana did for her group by speaking out on behalf of the sales support team in her meeting with the sales group. She then reinforces her message.

Dana: You've been a big help already. I know the sales support people will be pleased with what we've accomplished here. Thanks, not just from me, but from them as well. [*Dana provides*

them with an incentive to carry out their plans.]
Let's track what happens. If we keep transaction logs for two weeks, we'll be able to spot problems and deal with them proactively.

Directing

To become an effective leader, you have to provide people with direction and focus their energies on specific goals while maintaining high group morale. Dana accomplished that feat at the sales meeting; now she has to do the same with her own group. This again requires seeing the big picture, communicating goals and objectives to other people, and creating *synergy*—a focus on achieving the group goal in which everyone on the team has a stake.

Becoming Goal-Oriented: Seeing the big picture implies becoming goal-oriented. You can't provide direction unless, to paraphrase Lewis Carroll's Cheshire Cat, you know where you want people to go. You provide direction by identifying targets to achieve, setting deadlines for achieving them, and creating the conditions or means for getting the job done—the sum and substance of goal statements. And goal statements are the foundations of building action plans.

Communicating Goals and Objectives: A vision is a goal; the milestones for reaching the goal are objectives. To communicate your vision, you need to talk about goals and objectives clearly, succinctly, and enthusiastically. Dana does this at the meeting she has with her staff shortly after the sales meeting.

Dana: As you know, the meeting went very well, and we reached clear agreements and understandings. It now will take a great deal of goodwill and effort to execute the plans we came up with.

You and everyone at the meeting seem to agree on the same goal: to create more teamwork between us and the sales force. They appreciated your feedback, even if they didn't like all of it. You have a list of the objectives they came up with for this meeting, and I need to hear from each of you what you think of them. Then we can divvy up some assignments for implementing them or for amending them for further discussion with the sales department.

Goals and objectives—for the sales force, for the sales support team, for the meeting, and for follow-up to the meeting. All in four sentences.

Energizing: It takes both rational and emotional appeals to inspire people to strive toward their goals.

Patty [*dubious*]: Do you really think we can count on those bozos to follow through on this plan?

Dana [*laughing*]: Not if you continue to call them bozos.

Stan: Clods is more like it.

[*Dana's laughter dies in her throat. She knows people are still angry, but she didn't expect this much hostility. Her next speech is somewhat intense—perhaps, as Patty will later describe it, "mildly impassioned," but it betrays no trace of anger.*]

Dana: I'm going to have to ask you to give them a chance. Presuppose that they're bozos and clods, prejudge them, and it'll come across in your voices. They'll hear it. They'll resent it, and they'll come back at you in kind. Let's give them a chance. As I told you, until I laid it out for them, they didn't understand what you're

going through here. Now they're willing to
pitch in to help create the teamwork we all
want.

A plan based on carefully considered goals and objectives is the rational part of the leadership process.
The willingness to stand up for what's right is the emotional part. Together they create *synergy*—the focusing
of people's energies toward the accomplishment of a
commonly held goal.

Being a supervisor means having status power, a
condition that some people wear with grace and
warmth. Such people also have personal power, which
makes them effective leaders. Blessed are leaders who
have both status and personal power.

CHAPTER FIVE

Creating Synergy

It takes more than rational thought and emotional appeals to create and sustain synergy. If you are to become
a successful leader, you also have to manage the basic
elements of group dynamics that create successful
teams, that keep people focused on their goals, and that
keep groups cohesive: task and process dynamics.
These two separate but interactive forces drive *what*
people have to do and *how* they do it.

Task Dynamics

In a business environment, your goal—the achievement of the group's productivity goals—must always direct your thinking and your energies. This is true whether your goal is to produce a product, provide a service, or complete specific projects. The happiest, friendliest group in the world may not be successful when it comes to getting its work done, and that lack of success usually turns the group in on itself. The happy, friendly group then becomes a battleground in which disenchanted warriors self-destruct—one great moral of the King Arthur fable.

You, as a leader, can help any group to which you belong achieve its productivity goals through a variety of means that will keep the group focused on its objectives and directed toward achieving its goals. Only by doing what has to be done can the group get there. There are eighteen specific things you can do to lead people to accomplish their goals.

Ways to Facilitate Goal Achievement

Managing activities	Chairing meetings, facilitating meetings, and coordinating or managing resources
Initiating	Calling meetings, making suggestions, proposing new ideas, and getting activities started
Seeking information	Asking questions for clarification or to verify the accuracy of data
Giving information	Offering data and supplying printed or visual resources
Seeking opinions	Asking others for their views or their values or asking them to decide on the merits of an idea or a generalization
Expressing opinions	Stating your views, expressing your values, or deciding on the merits of an idea or a generalization

Brainstorming	Getting the group's information and opinions into the open and generating new or different ideas by asking participants to express ideas in a process that facilitates creativity and innovation
Elaborating	Interpreting, explaining, or explicating facts or opinions and drawing conclusions from the data available
Shaping or orienting	Identifying progress toward goals, defining positions, or organizing activity
Summarizing	Pulling together the group's suggestions during a meeting and pulling together related ideas or opinions by restating them or by coordinating activities of subgroups or group members
Seeking consensus	Polling the group for its readiness to make decisions or to resolve disagreements
Taking consensus	Asking that a decision be made or that issues be resolved, so that the group has to formulate a position and agree to abide by its decisions. (Consensus taking is not voting; unanimity, even if temporary and for the sake of testing an idea's fruitfulness, is superior to majority rule. After everyone gets a hearing, all members have to be willing at least to try out a decision until it proves unworkable.)
Setting standards	Establishing criteria for evaluating ideas, opinions, decisions, products, or services
Evaluating	Measuring ideas, opinions, or products against standards
Producing	Doing the work of the group's mission, whether it be to produce something or offer services, and taking whatever

	steps are necessary to achieve the stated target
Reporting	Taking notes at meetings, writing production reports, providing subjective impressions, and communicating the information to the group and to others with a need to know
Representing	Communicating the group's progress, needs, decisions, or actions to those outside the group
Maintaining	Providing materials and performing routine tasks that keep the team functioning without a hitch, such as ordering raw materials in time to keep production up to standard

Playing any one role contributes to a group's ability to achieve its goals. Playing any combination of roles will help you develop into a genuine leader.

On the other hand, you must take care not to become so focused, so overly task-oriented—obsessed with getting the task done at any cost—that you drive people away from you. You could become *task-dysfunctional*.

You and everyone else can tell if that's happening. You find yourself driving yourself and everyone else to get things done, to meet or beat a deadline, to reduce waste, to eliminate errors. Everyone begins to feel ground down and burned out because nothing is more important than "making the numbers." Being the leader (and being led) loses its good feeling, loses its fun.

Process Dynamics

By paying attention to how people interact with one another and by playing a variety of process roles, you can curb any tendency you might develop toward becoming a task-oriented tyrant. You can also prevent your group from becoming task-dysfunctional. To keep relationships healthy, you have to take the lead in managing the group's process dynamics.

Some people call this kind of management the "maintenance function" because it helps people maintain their relationships with one another while achieving their task-oriented goals. Your job is to help people maintain their relationships by paying attention to *how* they achieve their objectives, *how* they relate to each other, and *how* they support the good feelings they have about one another, about the group, and about you.

This list of ten maintenance functions will help you take a leadership role in maintaining your group.

Ways to Maintain a Group

Gatekeeping	Taking an interest in other people's opinions or feelings, opening the channels of communication, and ensuring that everyone who wants to can express an opinion, whether anyone likes that opinion or not
Listening	Paying attention to what people say and do
Expediting	Crossing the line between task and process by keeping discussions or activities on track while encouraging everyone to contribute
Encouraging	Allowing everyone to participate, acknowledging what people say or do, and avoiding cutting off or putting down people or discounting what they say or do
Empowering	Enabling other people to make decisions and to do things for themselves
Harmonizing	Negotiating, reconciling, or mediating disagreements and relieving tension with appropriate humor

Yielding	Giving up an unpopular viewpoint for the team's sake, not dominating the team even if you have status power, admitting to weaknesses or areas in need of improvement, and meeting people halfway
Observing	Looking and listening, alerting people to possible damage to effective functioning, expressing feelings you see in the group ("mirroring"), calling attention to group reactions to what is going on, and diagnosing problems reflected in group behavior
Accepting	Respecting people's right to express themselves and to meet their own needs, respecting and even promoting differences among people in order to begin a rational problem-solving process, and acknowledging people's shortcomings without being judgmental
Cheerleading	Helping people feel good about themselves, about the group functioning, and about the successes of individuals or the group, and urging people to achieve their goals or to improve their performance

Just as you can become task-dysfunctional, you can become overly process-oriented, or *process-dysfunctional*. You can become too passive during disagreements and let them rage around you without placing appropriate limits on discussion. You can avoid disagreements or suppress them by using status power inappropriately. You can create a country-club environment in which people enjoy their time together but accomplish nothing. You can ignore standards and avoid evaluating ideas, opinions, or products in an effort not to offend anyone. You can let brainstorming substitute for consensus taking and decision making. Good feelings then replace good results.

Pulling the Dynamics Together

We've seen Dana take many constructive steps as the leader of the sales support team. She provided her group with information. She sought information from various sources. She sought opinions from her group and from the sales force, and she expressed her own ideas. She played the role of gatekeeper by asking her group for its opinions and feelings; she played the same role by asking the salespeople how her group could help them the most. She then reconciled their differences by telling the salespeople what the support group could or could not do. She harmonized the relationships between the two groups and reconciled their differences. She yielded her status power by letting her group make suggestions and decisions. She encouraged people to do things—including to lay themselves off.

No one person can do all the things we listed all of the time, and you don't have to do all of them all of the time to be an effective leader. Empowering others helps you share leadership behaviors that anyone can adopt. If you have status power, you will enhance your personal power if you encourage other people to perform leadership roles as well.

Performing any combination of those roles will help you become a more effective leader. As you develop your skills and acquire the art of leadership, you will want to strive for a carefully poised balance between task and maintenance roles—shifting your emphasis from one to the other as the situation demands. People will see you do things that help them individually and that help the group, and they will come to admire your ability to get things done while keeping relationships between people healthy.

The more you help individuals succeed at what they do and the more you contribute to the group's overall results, in terms of both the goals it has to accomplish and the way in which it accomplishes them, the more likely people will perceive you as a leader, if not *the* leader. They may not tell you how much they appreciate what you've done, as Francine told Dana, but you'll know it by the effort they put out to meet the agenda you set forth.

CHAPTER SIX

How to Energize

᪉

To energize the group and to maintain its morale and enthusiasm, especially in the face of hardship, a leader needs to exhibit the kind of vitality that comes from a commitment to values, enthusiasm, and energy. Cheerleading is the least one can do to help the group keep itself going.

People often call this vitality the leader's "charisma." Originally a theological concept defined as a special spiritual gift, charisma has come to refer to an extraordinary power in a person, group, or cause that takes hold of popular imagination, and wins popular support. However, no one has been able to satisfactorily explain that special gift or that extraordinary power in

such a way that we can understand what it really is and how it works. We do know that three very specific behaviors are associated with effective leaders: a commitment to values, enthusiasm, and energy.

Commitment to Values

Effective leaders, charismatic leaders in particular, emotionally express a deep commitment to their own and their group's values. This deeply felt commitment gives rise to scores of clichés, especially in sports analogies.

Managing during tough times is as hard on managers (including first-line supervisors) as it is on nonmanagers. Here's where the rubber meets the road, as they say. The friction can burn you out unless you keep focused on the group's goals and believe that (1) they're right, (2) they're achievable, (3) they're realistic, and (4) this group in particular can achieve them. You must believe that, even if it takes all the reserves of energy and commitment you and the group have, you can succeed if you all pull together. The ability to embody these attitudes during tough times and to encourage them in others is what separates leaders from administrators and from followers.

Sports analogies abound when people talk about leadership, because in sports you find all the ingredients of leadership we've been describing: having a vision, focusing on goals, meeting objectives, rallying one's own strength and urging others on to greater heights when everything seems darkest.

Athletes have a commitment to values that calls out the best in them. They become focused on what's important to them and to the people depending on them for leadership. That's why values have become such an important political issue in recent years. The 1972 Watergate scandal and all its chicanery made it clear to the electorate that lying, cheating, stonewalling—all bespeaking a lack of integrity—can't be tolerated. So, too, in your own business environment. Get caught lying or double-dealing one time, and you undermine your bid for leadership. Get caught twice, and you're finished.

A commitment to values does *not* mean a fixation on goals—especially short-term objectives. Goals and objectives are derivative paths for realizing values, and there are as many different ways to reach goals as there are roads leading to Rome. To be an effective leader, you may have to hold steadfastly to your values while being flexible about the means for realizing them. The ends may not always justify the means, but they should always control them.

Dana understands these points clearly. While talking with her manager, Stu, she outlines both her new plans and her reasons for taking the new direction. Here's the end of their conversation and how she sums up her thoughts.

Stu seems pleased with everything he and Dana have discussed up to this point.

Stu: Your group's worked as hard as any in the company. I agree with you that the group is doing a great job with little help from us, but the reality is that they're still way off their numbers. I like what you've outlined; so, let's sum it up and get on with the day.

Dana: You were at the meeting, so I don't have to spell out all the details. But, in sum, the new direction I'm taking will take some patience on everyone's part.

Stu, we can't be all things to all people, and we have to set priorities. I'm going to let my group do that this afternoon. I've sent everyone the notes I took at the meeting. You have your copy in my report. I've called a meeting with a published agenda in order to give people a chance to think about these issues and to come up with what they see the priorities are. We'll satisfy all our productivity requirements, but we have to find new ways of doing that while satisfying the demands of our customers—including the salespeople—without punishing our people in return for their all-out effort. Goodwill does affect bottom line.

Dana's commitment to values is clear in her last two sentences. Reread them. They say a great deal about her.

Enthusiasm

Think of enthusiasm as a length of string. There it is on the floor. On its own, it lies there, curled up, limp and useless.

Give it a little tug, and the string straightens out. Pull at both ends, and the string grows straighter, tauter. Twang on it, and it hums.

Pull too hard, and the string stretches to the breaking point—and, if you're not careful, it snaps. Then you're back to where you started, with the string lying curled up on the floor, limp and useless. Only now there's less of it with which to start again.

If you aspire to leadership, you have to feel about life, about the group, and about its vision and mission the way successful leaders feel. They exhibit enthusiasm for life itself, for the group, and for the group's vision and missions.

Don't go off into La-la Land. That's what breaks the string. But take an optimistic view—what we call realistic optimism—recognizing the difficulties of a situation while remaining true to your values and goals.

Dana explains at the start of her next meeting with

the sales support staff that their numbers aren't good. Customer calls handled (that is, resolved satisfactorily) are down from last year at this time, even though incoming calls are greater. Salespeople's complaints are still higher than last year.

Dana: We knew this would happen, so I'm not surprised, even though I'm not satisfied with the results. The upside of it all is that if we look at the numbers over the last three months instead of comparing them to last year's, there's a steady improvement.

Patty: The salespeople are a lot more patient.

Francine: That helps.

Stan: We also just finished installing the phone message handler.

Dana [*smiling*]: I appreciate all of that, and that's what makes these numbers more upbeat. I explained that to Stu this morning, and he agreed with me that you are doing a great job. We want to get better, but we're not doing badly.

Realistic. This is what our world is like, Dana has told the group.

Unsatisfied. It can be better.

Optimistic. It will get better.

She's keeping the string taut, but not so taut that it breaks. Fortunately, she's not the type you often see dashing into the office on Monday morning, all aglow with exuberance, pawing at the dirt like a high-strung racehorse. "I'm excited! Life's not a bowl of cherries; it's a magnum of champagne. Let's go get 'em. We can do it. Let me at 'em. Rarin' to go! Rah! Rah! Rah! Kill! Kill! Kill!" That may work in the locker room, but hardly ever in the workplace. The only one you want to kill is the messenger.

Realistic optimism: knowing what you're up

against but believing in your ability, and the abilities of other people, to win. That's what informs enthusiasm, shapes it, gives it life.

Energy

The morning you punch the snooze alarm three times more than usual, drag yourself out of the bed, stumble over to the coffeepot, and stand in the shower until your skin wrinkles and you look like a prune—not wanting to face the day—that's the morning you know you're in trouble. That's the morning when it seems that only superhuman heroics will get you through the day. That's also the morning you have to call upon all the physical and emotional energies you have, because if you're the leader and you can't make it, who can?

Leaders have the energy necessary for conducting the business of the group and for withstanding the stresses and hardships of that business. Getting to work on time or early, staying on the job until quitting time or later, getting done what has to get done—those behaviors model what you expect from others and what you yourself are willing to do. Stamina comes from an effective personal regimen and is reinforced by commitment.

Personal Regimen: No two people are alike, so what works for me may not work for you and what works for you may not work for the people around you. Still, there are three basic steps for energizing yourself: Get moderate exercise, eat a balanced diet, and get enough rest.

When things get tough, what do you think gets sacrificed first? You've got it. Exercise, diet, and rest.

Long hours substitue for moderate exercise ("I've no time for that"). A called-in pizza replaces a solid lunch high in fiber and low in fat ("I've no time for that"). Constant grind pushes aside rest ("I've no time for that").

And if you smoke, you smoke more than usual. If you drink alcohol, you drink more than usual. You become ill-tempered, impatient, excitable, and frazzled. You may meet one deadline but fall behind on the next one because you don't have the energy to sustain you past the first one and because you've probably lost the support of your most productive people.

Reversing that pattern takes an effort, but in the long run the effort is worth it on three levels. One, you'll feel better. Two, you'll last longer and accomplish more. Three, your vigor and vitality will inspire others to do as you do.

Five minutes of stretching exercises followed by a brisk forty-minute walk three or four days a week will do more to restore your energy than anything else you can do. Are you a morning person? Do it when you get up. Are you an evening person? Do it just before dinner. Neither? Do it at noon instead of calling in that pizza.

Eat a good breakfast of cereal, skim milk, toast, and orange juice or fruit. (Stay away from fried eggs and bacon; they don't supply as much energy as you think, and they'll clog your arteries, to boot.) A moderate lunch high in fiber and carbohydrates will give you the zest you'll need for the balance of the day. Okay, if you have to, eat it at your desk, but it's better if you push away from the desk for an hour.

Rest and exercise go hand in hand. But how can you rest if the deadline is glaring at you from across tomorrow?

For ten minutes after your walk, if you walk at noon or after lunch if you stop for it, sit quietly *doing nothing*. You don't have to get into transcendental meditation to rest. Just deep relaxation will do. Listen to your own breathing with your eyes closed. If you have the time as well as the opportunity, snooze for a few minutes. A midday siesta is not just a cultural idiosyncrasy in southern Europe and other hot climates. It's a biological urge that, if satisfied, will revitalize your whole being. An hour with no productivity will increase your overall productivity by a significant factor. (Just how large the factor is depends on you and the kind of work you do.)

These steps provide emotional revitalization, as well as physical. Exercise, diet, and rest all affect how you feel *about* things as well as how you feel. It's hard to stay committed to your values and your goals when you're feeling terrible. You're more likely to give up if you feel tired or listless. A tired Casey never makes it up to the plate.

Commitment as Reinforcement: What's important to you can drive you past your apparent levels of endurance. That's the message from anyone who's returned from captivity in war or from being kidnapped in the Middle East. Thinking beyond the moment kept them alive, capable of enduring and willing to endure whatever hardship they experienced. Commitment energizes and reinforces the energy you need for pushing past what you think your limits are. Indeed, energy and commitment are reciprocal: The more energy you feel, the more commitment you feel; the more commitment you feel, the more energy you feel.

All this shows in what you do. You don't have to shout "I'm excited!" for the world to know it. Just do things with an air of excitement (without becoming hyper or manic in the process). If people believe you're a leader, they will strive to emulate what they see in you.

If you're a leader, the vigor and energy you need to accomplish your tasks will come only from your commitment to your goal. Your feelings about the need to comply with the demands of other people or with the demands of a situation will show in the way you attack your tasks or the issues at hand. Grudging obedience will show in the desultory way you go about your obvious drudgery. These attitudes, in turn, will affect what you can expect from others—regardless of what you tell them.

Emotions are a form of energy. Feel good about what you are doing, submerge yourself in its rightness, and your feelings will show. The emotions embodied in an orator's delivery makes what that person says important, as well as memorable. The difference between "We *have* to meet our productivity goals" and "We *can* meet our productivity goals" is not just a matter of words. The emotional connotations of the words deliver the message. "I have a dream" means little without the passion in Martin Luther King, Jr.'s voice. The delivery carried the emotion that led America to share the dream.

Values, enthusiasm, and energy—maybe that's all there is to charisma. And you, as much as anyone else, can have a commitment to what's important to you, feel excited about it, and have the energy to go for the gold.

Conclusion

Everyone can become a leader, but not everyone will. It takes an often unspoken agreement between two or more people to form an alliance in which one is identified as the leader and the other, the follower. Since it is an agreement, it also requires that each person get something out of the relationship. "I'll recognize you as the leader," I say, "as long you do things that in the long run are in my interest as well as in yours." "Yes," you answer. And, thus, a leader is created.

From this point on, your destiny as a leader is in your own hands. Your job is to sustain your image so that, in my perception, you exemplify the traits of leadership I expect of you, that you hold beliefs, values, or attitudes to which I can respond positively, and that you do things that I can admire and would emulate if I could. That means that you have to act like a leader, or else I will stop believing in you and stop following you. At that point, you'll be my leader no more.

To sustain your image in my perception, you have to have a vision of what could be, as opposed to what is. You have to communicate your vision of the big picture, of how everything comes together to form a single whole. That's difficult for most people to see unless someone articulates it for them. That's your job as a leader.

When you articulate that vision, you have to ensure that you interpret and articulate my needs, aspirations, and feelings, as well as your own. I have to see me in that vision, or I can't make the vision mine. As for me, so, too, for everyone else in our group and for the group as a whole. Unless we can see ourselves in the picture, you'll find yourself alone as you charge the hill.

And charging the hill is what leadership is all about—goals to achieve, barriers to conquer, end results to produce. I and the group need you to help us understand what to do and how to do it, but, beyond that, we need you to communicate our needs, aspirations, and feelings to other people. No one will listen if we all gather in the CEO's office to make our case, but the CEO will listen if you represent us well. Besides, most of us haven't practiced the skills of leadership that would enable us to do it for ourselves.

Especially during tough times, we need you to encourage us to do what seems impossible to do. We need to feel that you respect us and care for what we need or want, that you respect us for who we are as well as for what we can do. In return, we will respect you.

We need direction and focus, or we'll dissipate our energies. People do that too often. Plato called democracy the form of government in which the people's emotions run amok. Everyone wants to know "what's in it for me"; we need you to provide direction and to channel our energies in the direction of doing the right thing.

Your enthusiasm for that vision, for its goals and objectives, will lift our morale when times are toughest. If your passion for the vision, for change, for growth, or for improvement flags, ours will flag as well. Your energy invests the group with a total energy that no one person alone can muster. Call it charisma, if you like.

Vision, communication, concern, respect, enthusiasm, energy—these are the ingredients of synergy. You and all the other people in our group create the synergy that makes our group successful. By performing the task and process roles appropriate to the group's needs and wishes, you become a leader.

As all those sports metaphors for leadership say, it takes practice, practice, practice—and everyone can become a leader if he or she chooses to do so.

Am I Already a Leader?

❧

Instructions: On the spaces provided, answer YES or NO to each item in this unscientific but useful survey. Then read the interpretations to determine whether you are already doing the things that people do to distinguish themselves as leaders.

___ 1. It's important to me that individuals in the group get what they need or want for themselves.

___ 2. When I look at a situation, I look for more than what affects me immediately and directly.

___ 3. When I talk with people about what we are doing or how we are doing it, I relate what I'm saying to the group's needs, aspirations, and feelings.

___ 4. When dealing with a problem, I look for the wider implications of what I know or believe.

___ 5. I attack everything I do with vigor and a willingness to give it my all.

___ 6. I get excited by new challenges presented to the group.

___ 7. I represent my group to people outside it in such a way that they can understand what the group wants or needs to be successful.

___ 8. I spend as much time as I can afford helping build people's morale, especially when they feel down or are not receiving what they think they deserve.

___ 9. When talking with other people about situations that affect us, I try to explain how I see the relationships between us and other people or between us and the organization as a whole.

___10. Usually, I express the group's needs, aspirations, and feelings more clearly than and more thoroughly than most other people in the group.

___11. I keep myself physically and emotionally fit and feel vigorous most of the time.

___12. People are more than mere instruments or tools for meeting my objectives or the goals of the organization.

___13. As often as I can, I encourage people to act on the basis of long-term goals, rather than on the basis of immediate returns.

___14. I care about how people in the group feel or what they want for themselves.

___15. I feel good about what we're doing and how we're doing it.

___16. I believe that anything can be improved, and I welcome change.

___17. I help people see where we're going and how we're trying to get there.

___18. It's important to me that the group fulfill its goals and meet its needs.

___19. I know we can do better than we are doing, and I will do whatever it takes to make it better.

___20. The people with whom I associate are important to me and have my respect.

___21. Whenever I get the chance, I talk with other people about how the group is doing, what it wants, or what it needs to be successful.

___22. Whenever the situation seems confused or dismal, I encourage people to look forward toward the future and to concentrate on achieving our goals or objectives.

Interpretations: Each trait of leadership listed in Chapter

1 is represented by a pair of statements. Add up your YES and NO responses. If you answered YES to every item, you're already a super leader (or you're kidding yourself). If you answered YES to most of the items, you're on your way to being a superior leader. If you answered YES and NO equally, you're somewhat confused as to how to be a leader, and this book will help you improve the quality of your leadership. If you answered NO to most of them, you're either underestimating yourself grossly or you have a long way to go toward becoming an effective leader, and this book could help you.

- The ability to see the whole picture
  2. When I look at a situation, I look for more than what affects me immediately and directly.
  4. When dealing with a problem, I look for the wider implications of what I know or believe.

- The ability to communicate the whole picture to other people
  9. When talking with other people about situations that affect us, I try to explain how I see the relationships between us and other people or between us and the organization as a whole.
  13. As often as I can, I encourage people to act on the basis of long-term goals, rather than on the basis of immediate returns.

- The ability to interpret and articulate the group's needs, aspirations, and feelings
  3. When I talk with people about what we are doing or how we are doing it, I relate what I'm saying to the group's needs, aspirations, and feelings.
  10. Usually, I express the group's needs, aspirations, and feelings more clearly and more thoroughly than most other people in the group.

- Concern for the needs, aspirations, and feelings within the group

    14. I care about how people in the group feel or what they want for themselves.
    18. It's important to me that the group fulfill its goals and meet its needs.

- Respect for the needs, aspirations, feelings, and abilities within the group

    20. The people with whom I associate are important to me and have my respect.
    12. People are more than mere instruments or tools for meeting my objectives or the goals of the organization.

- The ability to communicate the group's needs, aspirations, and feelings for, to, and outside the group

    21. Whenever I get the chance, I talk with other people about how the group is doing, what it wants, or what it needs to be successful.
    7. I represent my group to people outside it in such a way that they can understand what the group wants or needs to be successful.

- A grasp of what people need or want for themselves that will encourage them to do what they otherwise might not do for themselves or for others

    1. It's important to me that individuals in the group get what they need or want for themselves.
    8. I spend as much time as I can afford helping build people's morale, especially when they feel down or are not receiving what they think they deserve.

- The ability to provide people with direction and to focus their energies on specific goals while maintaining a high group morale

22. Whenever the situation seems confused or dismal, I encourage people to look forward toward the future and to concentrate on achieving our goals or objectives.
17. I help people see where we're going and how we're trying to get there.

- Enthusiasm for the group's mission, objectives, and standards
  15. I feel good about what we're doing and how we're doing it.
  6. I get excited by new challenges presented to the group.

- An avid desire for change, growth, or improvement
  19. I know we can do better than we are doing, and I will do whatever it takes to make it better.
  16. I believe that anything can be improved, and I welcome change.

- The energy necessary for conducting the business of the group
  11. I keep myself physically and emotionally fit and feel vigorous most of the time.
  5. I attack everything I do with vigor and a willingness to give it my all.

Suggested Readings

Avolio, B. J., and Bernard M. Bass. "Transformation Leadership, Charisma and Beyond." In J. G. Hunt et al., eds. *Emerging Leadership Vistas*. Lexington, Mass.: Lexington Books, 1988.

Bennis, Warren, with Burt Nanus. *Leaders: The Strategies for Taking Charge*. New York: Harper & Row, 1985.

————. *Unconscious Conspiracy: Why Leaders Can't Lead*. New York: AMACOM, 1976.

Korda, Michael. *Power! How To Get It, How To Use It*. New York: Random House, 1975.

Peters, Tom. *Thriving on Chaos: Handbook for a Management Revolution*. New York: Alfred A. Knopf, 1988.

Senge, Peter M. *The Fifth Discipline: The Art and Practice of The Learning Organization*. New York: Doubleday Currency, 1986.

Tannenbaum, Robert, and Warren H. Schmidt. "How to Choose a Leadership Pattern." *Harvard Business Review* (May–June 1973), pp. 162ff.

Waterman, Robert H. *The Renewal Factor: How the Best Get and Keep the Competitive Edge*. New York: Bantam Books, 1987.

Weiss, Donald H. *How to Build High Performance Teams*. Watertown, Mass.: American Management Association, 1991.

Index

❧

About the Author

Donald H. Weiss, Ph.D., is CEO of Self-Management Communications, Inc., St. Louis, and a well-known author of books, videos, and cassette-workbook programs that focus on management and interpersonal skills. He has been a senior training and development executive and consultant for more than twenty-five years. Among his corporate positions were: program manager for the Citicorp Executive Development Center and corporate training manager for Millers' Mutual Insurance. His many publications include fifteen previous books in the SOS series and *Fair, Square, and Legal: Safe Hiring, Managing, and Firing Practices to Keep Your Company Out of Court* (all AMACOM). Dr. Weiss earned his Ph.D. from Tulane University.